Unhinged:

The Shocking True Story of Ed Gein

Robert Keller

Please Leave Your Review of This Book At
http://bit.ly/kellerbooks

ISBN-13: 978-1548732257

ISBN-10: 1548732257

© 2017 by Robert Keller

robertkellerauthor.com

Table of Contents

Unhinged: The Shocking Story of Ed Gein

The unknown killer had been dubbed Buffalo Bill because, as one rookie FBI agent indelicately put it, "he skins his hides." Like most serial killers, Bill had a preferred victim type. He targeted big-boned, slightly obese, young women. Already three had died, their bodies bearing bizarre mutilations. Large strips of skin had been carefully sliced from each of the corpses and apparently carried away by the killer.

No one knew for certain why Bill had cut his victims in this way. That horrific realization would come only later when the police finally tracked him down. It appeared that he'd been using the skin to make for himself a suit of clothing, a female body suit which he had spent hours lovingly stitching together and which he'd wear whenever the mood took him.

The story described above is, of course, fictional. It is the main subplot in the Thomas Harris thriller, The Silence of the Lambs, and its subsequent movie adaptation. Buffalo Bill, however, is not entirely a construct of the author's imagination. He is based on a real person, a shy, slight and apparently harmless Wisconsin farmer named Ed Gein.

To the citizens of Plainfield, the tiny hamlet that will forever be associated with Gein's horrific deeds, Ed was a figure who inspired both disdain and pity. The unkempt and slightly addled-brained bachelor had grown up in the area but had always kept himself apart from the other residents. As a child, that isolation had been enforced by his dominant, Bible-punching mother. But Ed had remained on the periphery, even after his mother's passing. His only interaction with the other townsfolk was when he hired himself out as a handyman or served as a babysitter for their children.

For the most part, Gein remained ensconced at his ramshackle farmhouse, a building that had acquired a reputation among the local kids as haunted. The adults chuckled when they heard stories about Ed's shrunken head collection or about the corpse-like figure that had been spotted dancing naked in the moonlight on his property. Ed, they knew, was obsessed with the macabre and had probably bought the artifacts at some Halloween store in Lacrosse.

It was only later that the dreadful truth was revealed, only later that they learned about the dark deeds that had been committed on the Gein farm. The children of Plainfield had been right all along. A monster had been living in their midst.

Chapter 1: The Road to Plainfield

The village of Plainfield, Wisconsin sits in the northwest corner of Waushara County, in a locale that is about as close as it is possible to get to the center of the Beaver State. The name Plainfield is descriptive of the town and indeed of the region, a nondescript and featureless landscape with the flatness of a billiard table. This is farming country, uplifted in recent times by the introduction of modern agricultural methods and equipment. When our story takes place, however, in the 1940s and 50s, few farmers were able to eke out more than a subsistence living here. The soil was dry and stony, fit only for the cultivation of rye, and of potatoes more suited to starch production than to human consumption. Most of the area's farming folk turned their efforts instead to raising dairy cattle.

Having painted such a depressing picture of our location, it would be fair to ask why anyone would be drawn to live in such a desolate place. In truth, few were. Throughout its history, the population of Plainfield has never challenged the 1,000 mark. Back in the forties, it hovered around 600 hardy souls, among them the Gein family, who lived on a one-hundred-ninety-five-acre spread some miles outside of town. The Geins had purchased the property in 1914 but had made little effort in the ensuing decades to integrate into the community. In fact, they appeared determined to avoid their fellow Plainfielders at all costs, a stance driven in the main by the family matriarch, Augusta Wilhelmine Lehrke Gein.

Augusta was a formidable woman, the product of strict Lutheran parents who had immigrated from Germany in 1870 and settled in La Crosse, Wisconsin. A coarse-featured and heavy-set woman, she was hardly the type to set a man's heart aflutter. Add to that her near fanatical adherence to the holy texts and it is easy to see why she'd reached her twentieth year before the first potential suitor put in an appearance. His name was George Gein and he was an orphan, having lost his parents and older sister to a flash flood when he was still a toddler.

George had been raised by his maternal grandparents, stern Scottish immigrants who gave him little affection but plenty of discipline. He'd received just an elementary school education before being apprenticed to a blacksmith, a trade he apparently despised and soon abandoned. Thereafter, he moved to the nearest big town, La Crosse, and worked at various jobs while also developing a taste for alcohol. It was while employed at the David, Medary & Platz Tannery that George met Fred Lehrke. Soon after, Fred introduced George to his cousin Augusta.

On the face of it, George and Augusta made an unlikely pair. Augusta, even at 19, was a fiercely determined woman, set in her ways, judgmental, and entirely convinced that her religious worldview was the only one that mattered. George, on the other hand, was a weakling, prone to bouts of depression and self-recrimination, already well on the road to alcoholism in his early twenties.

And yet, the two were drawn to one another. For George, it was likely the expanded Lehrke clan, rather than Augusta herself, that proved attractive. Deprived of parental love and the company of siblings during his upbringing, he must have found the large and raucous family an enticing proposition.

As for Augusta, she was hardly beset by suitors and George was reasonably handsome and well presented. He was also a churchgoer, although not as fanatical as she regarding the Christian tenets. Perhaps she also saw in George the weakness that he detected in himself. Here was a man, Augusta must have decided, who she could bend to her will. Whatever the true circumstances of their courtship, George soon proposed and Augusta accepted. They were married on December 4, 1899, when Augusta was 19 and George was 23.

As most could have predicted, the marriage of George and Augusta Gein was not a happy one. Augusta quickly assumed the role of domestic tyrant, laying down the law and berating her husband at every opportunity for his laziness, weakness and lack of ambition. He, in turn, retreated, into himself and into the bottle, a habit that cost him more than one job and gave Augusta another stick to beat him with. When George inevitably reached the end of his tether and struck back, slapping his wife with an open hand, she'd fall to her knees and pray for his deliverance.

It seems unlikely, impossible even, that such a union might be blessed with children. But Augusta longed for a baby, even if the thought of carnal relations with her husband filled her with disgust. She had, by this time, already begun her long descent into pathological religious mania. To her, the world was populated by fallen women and La Crosse was the twin city of the biblical

Sodom and Gomorrah. Sexual intimacy, even within the context of a God-sanctioned marriage, must have seemed like an unspeakable depravity.

Still, she gritted her teeth and allowed her husband to perform the loathsome act upon her. She was relieved when she quickly fell pregnant and could eject him from her boudoir. Then she began planning the arrival of her firstborn. She prayed for a daughter who she could mold in her own image and raise as a pious, god-fearing woman. Instead, the Lord chose to give her a son and while Augusta accepted that as His divine will, she would never be close to the boy, Henry, born January 17, 1902.

With a child to support, George's work shy ways became more of an issue to Augusta. Previously, his inability to hold down a job had been a source of annoyance. Now, it had become a matter of the survival of their family. Her solution to the problem was to summarily inform her husband that they were starting their own business. Augusta's family, the Lehrkes, appear to have been quite entrepreneurial. Two of her brothers ran successful grocery stores and Augusta decided that she and George would start a similar business. In 1909, the couple acquired a lease on a small commercial property at 914 Caledonian Street and began trading.

George Gein, however, had no more talent for entrepreneurship than he had for being a salaried employee. The business was soon in trouble, requiring Augusta to step in and rescue the situation. Within eighteen months she had assumed the twin roles of proprietress and bookkeeper, relegating her husband to packing shelves, bagging groceries and making deliveries.

In late 1905, Augusta again allowed her husband into her bed. The act of copulation was as disgusting to her as ever but she steeled herself and bore it in the hope of conceiving the daughter she had always wanted. From the moment she realized that she was pregnant, she began praying nightly for the little girl she so craved. But again, her wishes were denied. On August 27, 1906, she delivered another son, a cherub-cheeked infant who she named Edward Theodore Gein.

Chapter 2: Eddie

Ed Gein, or Eddie as he was affectionately known, grew up to be a slight and sensitive boy, beholden to his mother in all things. It would be safe to say that he worshiped the ground she walked on. She was the rock in the family, running both the business and the household while her poor excuse for a husband cowered stoop-shouldered in her wake. Even as a boy, Eddie and his brother Henry had very little time for George Gein, who only seemed to notice their presence when he was drunk and felt that they needed "putting straight" with his leather belt.

Then, in 1913, came a major change in young Eddie's life. Augusta had long bemoaned the "evils" of city living and had spoken often of taking her sons away from its temptations to a simpler life in the country. Over the years of running her grocery store she had diligently squirreled away a percentage of the profits and had now accumulated enough money to bring her dream to fruition. George, as always, had no say in the matter. Augusta simply announced that they were selling the business and that was that.

Late that year, the Geins packed up their belongings and moved forty miles east of La Crosse, to a small dairy farm that Augusta had purchased near Camp Douglas. But, for whatever reason, the farm did not meet Augusta's exacting standards and within a year she had sold up and acquired a bigger plot of land near Plainfield.

The property included an attractive white-frame homestead, built in an L-configuration over two stories. The outbuildings included a large barn, a chicken coop and an equipment shed. The previous owner had also built a summer kitchen onto one side of the house, connected via an inter-leading door to the regular kitchen. All-in-all it was pleasing to the house-proud Augusta and she quickly got to work turning it into a home for her family. Pride of place was reserved for a large painting of Christ gazing skyward towards heaven.

There was one other feature of her new homestead that met with Augusta Gein's approval – its isolation. The nearest neighbors, the Johnsons, were a quarter mile away and the nearest town, Plainfield, was a six-mile journey over rutted dirt roads. This suited Augusta just fine. She had no desire to interact with the locals, who she had already prejudged as being of low moral fiber. Trips into town would be made only out of absolute necessity. Other than that, she and her brood would remain sequestered at their farmstead, free of the corrupting influences of the world.

But of course, Augusta could not isolate her family entirely. Henry and Eddie had to attend school. When Eddie was eight, he was enrolled at the Roche-a-Cri grade school, where he was one of just a dozen students. Later, Roche-a-Cri merged with the White School and it was there, at age 16, that Eddie completed his formal education. He was a good, if unexceptional, student who loved to read. Early on he developed a taste for macabre comic books like "Tales from the Crypt" and for stories of headhunters, cannibals and Nazi atrocities. His mother, of course, would have been horrified at her son consuming such "evil works" but Eddie was able to keep that knowledge from her. Had Augusta discovered his taste in reading material and forbade him from it, his life might well have taken a different trajectory.

Eddie's school years were not a happy time. He found it difficult to interact with his peers, ever wary of his mother's warnings about "other people." On the few occasions that he did strike up a friendship with one of his classmates, Augusta would nip it in the bud, instructing him to immediately stop associating with the boy and calling him a fool for doing so in the first place. On these occasions, Eddie would be reduced to a flood of tears and heartfelt apology. At school the following day, he'd completely blank his new friend, ignoring his questions and refusing even to make eye contact.

Children, of course, can be extremely cruel towards anyone they consider "different." But while Eddie's classmates did perceive some of his behavior as odd (the peculiar lopsided grin he always wore, for example) it appears that he was not a particular target for schoolyard bullies. On the one occasion that some kid did tease him, about a fleshy growth on his left eyelid that caused the eye to sag, Eddie broke down in tears and ran away. That incident served only to highlight to Ed that his mother was right, that the world was a harsh place and that people were inherently mean.

Back at the Gein homestead, meanwhile, Augusta's dreams of operating a prosperous farm had run aground on the sandy soil of Waushara County. Despite all of their hard work, the ground yielded barely enough crops for their own consumption. And George was no longer any use around the place. He'd long since lost himself in his alcoholism and his growing melancholia. His time was spent mainly loafing, drinking himself into a stupor and ranting at his wife and children all of whom regarded him with barely disguised disdain.

George's drinking and his refusal to work had put a heavy burden on Augusta and her sons. The wise course of action would probably have been to abandon their infertile land but Augusta refused to countenance such an idea. Instead, she and her sons picked up the cudgel. The boys had both grown into strapping teenagers, short in stature but wiry and strong, with their mother's appetite for hard work.

Since Augusta by now refused to go into Plainfield at all, one of the boys' duties was to make the weekly provision run into town. But their mother seldom allowed them to depart without delivering one of her lectures. They were not to associate with anyone other than to transact their business. And they were particularly to avoid women who, with their powders and lipstick, were the spawn of Satan. Women would lead them from the path of righteousness, she cautioned.

And these religious outpourings were not confined to the provisioning run either. Every night, as George slumped passed out in his chair, Augusta would gather her boys around her to read from the good book. Her favorite passages were those of the fire and brimstone variety, particularly the one's that spoke on her favorite subject, the wantonness of women. Afterwards, she would take both of the boys by the hand and make them swear that they would remain pure. If their lust became too overpowering, she said, then the sin of Onan (masturbation) was preferable to fornication. The message quite obviously got through. Neither Ed nor Henry would ever marry or even attempt to court a girl.

Chapter 3: Murder One?

George Gein had endured a hard and largely cheerless existence. Orphaned as a toddler, raised by grandparents who showed him little affection, married to a woman who clearly detested him, George had derived his only succor in life from the narrow end of a whiskey bottle. But his heavy drinking had taken a toll. By his early sixties, he was a helpless invalid, entirely dependent on a family who thought he'd be better off dead and sometimes told him so. In 1937, when George was 66, he granted their wish, succumbing to a heart attack. He was buried at the Plainfield Methodist church on April 4.

After George's passing, the Gein family quickly fell back to its workaday routine on the farm. If anything, their lives were made easier, since they no longer had to care for the old man. But in 1942, a new threat to their livelihood emerged. War had been raging in Europe for four years and now the United States had entered the conflict. That meant conscription for men of a certain age and Ed, at 36, fell within that bracket. That would have left his mother desperately short-handed.

As expected, a letter duly arrived summoning Ed to a medical in Milwaukee, a journey of 136 miles which would be the longest Ed Gein made in his entire life. Fortunately for him (and for Augusta) the draft board turned Ed down, due to impaired vision in his left eye. He returned to Plainfield where in addition to his farm duties he now earned money doing odd jobs. The income from these jobs was essential to the family's survival as it had long since become evident that the farm's tainted soil was never going to provide them with a living.

Another source of income for Ed was babysitting. Ed was good with kids and he was popular with their parents, always polite, always diffident. The kids loved him and he seemed to have a real rapport with them, more so than he'd ever had with people of his own age. He was particularly skilled as a story teller and would enthrall his young charges with creepy tales of South Sea cannibals and headhunters. Ed knew a lot about the subject, of course. He'd been entranced by such stories since he was a boy himself.

Henry Gein also spent a lot of his time doing paid work away from the farm. Of the two, Henry was the more outgoing, the more at ease with outside folk. This was probably because, unlike Ed, Henry did not take everything his mother said as gospel. It was something that occasionally came between them, when Ed challenged Henry on some or other comment he'd made about Augusta which Ed considered less than respectful. Still, those issues were usually resolved quickly once Henry assured Ed that he loved their mother deeply and had nothing but respect and admiration for her. That usually set Ed's mind at rest. He was close to Henry and looked up to him. If it were ever to come down to a choice between him and their mother, though, there could only be one winner.

Which brings us to the subject of Henry's tragic and unexpected death at the age of just 43. It happened on Tuesday, May 16, 1944, while the Gein brothers were fighting a runaway brush fire on their property. No one knows how the fire started exactly. In some versions of the story it began accidentally, in others, the brothers set it deliberately to burn off the dry grass. Whatever the case, a strong wind picked up and began directing the flames towards a stand of pines at one end of the field.

The brothers quickly realized that they could not allow the flames to reach the trees and set off a much larger conflagration. They therefore decided to split their firefighting efforts, with Ed circling around to attack the blaze from the south while his brother continued working the northern edge. By this time, the smoke was so thick that Ed soon lost sight of Henry. Nonetheless, he continued to beat at the bushes with damp hessian bags, continued to hastily construct firebreaks with his shovel. Eventually, exhausted, his face blackened by soot, he'd gained the upper hand.

By now it was dark and Ed had not seen Henry for several hours. He could see, however, that his brother had also been successful in putting out his side of the fire. All that lay before him was a field of embers, glowering in the dark. Ed walked directly across them, calling out to Henry but getting no response. He then jogged back to the farmhouse expecting that Henry would be there. He wasn't.

Concerned now, Ed ran back to the field and continued searching for his brother but found nothing. Eventually, after about an hour, he decided that he needed to get help and drove in his truck to his neighbors, the Johnsons. They, in turn, summoned Deputy Sherriff Frank Engle and a search party was hastily assembled.

Back at the field, Ed urged the men to follow him and then set off at pace, leading the group within minutes to the spot where Henry lay. This particularly concerned Deputy Engle. Hadn't Ed just told them that he'd been searching for over an hour and had been unable to find Henry? How then had he been able to lead them directly to the corpse? Engle let that anomaly slide for now. It was clear that Henry Gein was beyond help but the Deputy needed to make a quick in situ inspection of the body and its immediate vicinity.

But that inspection threw up a whole host of new questions about Henry Gein's death. The patch of ground on which he lay was scorched black and yet Henry appeared unharmed by the flames. The only marks on him appeared to be an array of peculiar bruises on his head, bruises that may or may not have been inflicted by someone wielding a shovel.

That, in any case, was not up to the deputy to resolve. The medical examiner would have to make a call as to cause of death. What Engle needed to know was how Ed had been able to lead them directly to the body when his earlier search had failed to locate Henry. He put that question to Ed now, while they awaited the arrival of the coroner's van. "Funny how that works," was all the little man would say, as though that explained everything.

Henry Gein's body was removed for autopsy where County Coroner George Bladder determined that he'd died of asphyxiation. As for the bruises on his head, Bladder thought that he might have struck his head on a rock when he collapsed after being overcome by the smoke. No one appears to have mentioned that the field in which the fire had occurred was not particularly rocky. Neither was any attempt made to locate the offending rock. How else might George have acquired his head injury? There was certainly no suggestion that his brother might have inflicted it upon him.

Chapter 4: Alone

Henry Gein was laid to rest beside his father in the Plainfield Cemetery. If Ed was particularly bereaved by his brother's passing he showed no outward sign of it. In public he continued to wear his disconcerting and permanently affixed smile. Expressions of condolence were accepted with a shrug of the shoulders and a resigned sigh, as if to say "it's done and can't be undone."

But Ed's response to the next misfortune to befall his family was rather more pronounced. One day, just a few months after Henry's death, Augusta complained of feeling unwell. Ed knew it was serious when his mother, who refused to leave the farm except in the most dire of circumstances, insisted that he take her to a doctor.

Augusta was taken to the hospital in the nearby town of Wild Rose. There, Ed spent an anxious few hours in the waiting room before a doctor appeared to solemnly inform him that his mother had suffered a stroke. Augusta would have to stay at the hospital and during that time, Ed became a fixture around the place, spending as much visitation time as he was allowed in the ward as well as many hours in the waiting area.

Eventually, Augusta was discharged and Ed transported her back to the farm where he put her to bed and over the weeks that followed tended to her every need. Augusta was a good patient. She seldom complained and provided Ed with all of the instructions he needed for her care. Chief among those was for him to sit with her in the evening reading from the bible by lamplight. Ed was grateful for the opportunity. He relished waiting on the woman he adored above all others. He was almost disappointed when, after months of bedrest, Augusta announced that she was ready to be on her feet again. That was in mid-1945 and Augusta Gein had less than six months to live.

On December 29, 1945, Augusta suffered another stroke and was rushed back to the Wild Rose Hospital where she died that same day of a brain hemorrhage. Ed Gein had lost the woman who had been the center of his universe for all of his 39 years.

To say that Ed was distraught at the death of his mother would be a massive understatement. He was destroyed by his loss, consumed by it. At the sparsely attended funeral he wailed so loudly that he drowned out the vicar. Later, at the cemetery, he stood with tears and snot running down his face as the casket was lowered into the ground. Then he said a tearful goodbye to the few family members who had bothered to show up and retreated back to the sanctuary of his farmhouse. He had never felt so alone. In fact, he doubted that he would be able to bear the weight of his sorrow.

But Ed did emerge from his grief. After a period of bereavement, he began slowly taking on odd jobs again. However deep his despair, he had to earn a living.

To the outside world, Ed seemed to change little after the death of his mother. He was still the same soft-spoken, awkward individual, he still wore his peculiar lopsided grin, he could still be called on to do a favor for anyone in need. It was true that his physical appearance, never that well-groomed to begin with, had deteriorated. And it was also evident to anyone who passed the Gein farmhouse that the old place had fallen rapidly into disrepair after Augusta's passing. Weeds now covered the once-tidy front yard, growing between rusty farm implements; the porch roof was sagging, the paint peeling from the walls; woodland was reclaiming the pastures in which rye had once been sown; the few cows the family had owned had been sold off. In truth, Ed had no need to work the farm. His needs were few and could be easily financed by leasing out some of his land and by doing odd jobs for his neighbors. Ed was a hard worker and a reliable one, so he was never out of employment.

As for his life away from work, Ed had none. He was the very picture of the lonely old bachelor, who retreated to the dubious comforts of his dilapidated farmhouse at the end of the day to do God-only-knew what. More than one of the farmers' wives in the area took pity on him and would sometimes deliver a home-cooked meal or a batch of cookies. Their menfolk, meanwhile, thought Ed odd. There was a distinctly feminine quality to him which some of them found disconcerting. And they also found his preferred topics of conversation to be weird.

Ed seldom had much to contribute to a discussion unless the subject veered towards the macabre and bizarre. Then he was difficult to shut up. He'd talk at length about how tribesmen on the South Pacific islands decapitated their enemies and kept their shrunken heads as souvenirs; how English body snatchers during the 19th century dug up corpses and sold them to medical researchers; and how one particular group of depraved English aristocrats exhumed the bodies of recently deceased young women for what Ed described as "indecent purposes." Another favorite subject was the atrocities committed by the Nazis. One story he particularly enjoyed telling was about how Ilse Koch, the so-called "Bitch of Buchenwald," made lampshades and other artifacts from the skin of murdered concentration camp inmates. Ed appeared almost breathless as he relayed the details of these outrages in graphic detail.

If there was one exception to Ed's routine during this time it was the regular visits he made to Mary Hogan's tavern in the neighboring town of Pine Grove. This was odd for a number of reasons. First, Ed wasn't much of a drinker, hardly surprising when you consider that he'd been raised by an alcoholic father and a mother who thought that whiskey and beer were pumped straight from the bowels of hell. Second, if Ed had been inclined to stop off for a drink, why make the 7-mile trek to Pine Grove, when there were any number of perfectly serviceable taverns closer at hand? It wasn't that the Hogan place offered any particular attraction. It was a concrete bunker topped by a curved corrugated iron roof, Spartan inside and run by an abrasive woman of dubious reputation.

It seems that Ed's real reason for visiting Hogan's was the proprietress herself. Mary Hogan was a stoutly-built, middle-aged woman who spoke with a thick German accent and was seldom able to complete a sentence without the insertion of several cuss words. And yet, Ed appeared fascinated by the thickset tavern owner. To him, she was the mirror image of his sainted mother, coarse where Augusta had been refined, profane where she had been pure. Ed would spend hours in the bar, nursing a single beer while directing wistful glances in Mary's direction. It was as though this woman, so like his mother in appearance, so unlike her in character, had cast a spell on him.

Chapter 5: The Missing

Over a ten-year period, beginning in the late 1940's, law officers in central Wisconsin were baffled by a number of mysterious disappearances from their jurisdictions. The first of these occurred on the Thursday afternoon of May 1, 1947. Eight-year-old Georgia Weckler had attended her grade school in Jefferson that day and had been lucky enough to get a ride home with her neighbor, Mrs. Floerke, sparing her a long walk on a warm day. Mrs. Floerke had dropped Georgia off at the end of her drive on Highway 12, leaving her with a half-mile walk to the Weckler farmhouse. She never made it.

When Georgia's parents finally realized that she was missing that evening, hundreds of volunteers assisted the police in searching an area of ten square miles around Jefferson, hoping to find the little girl. Unfortunately, those searches came up empty. The only clues to Georgia's disappearance were tire marks found near the place where she had last been seen.

Six years later, in La Crosse, Wisconsin, another young girl went missing under mysterious circumstances. Evelyn Hartley was a pretty 15-year-old and the daughter of Richard Hartley, a biology professor at Wisconsin State College. On the evening of Saturday, October 24, 1953, Evelyn was babysitting the 20-month-old daughter of her father's colleague, Professor Viggo Rasmussen.

Evelyn had only recently started babysitting and had set up a routine where she would phone her parents several times during the evening. On this evening, however, the calls failed to come.

At around 9 a.m., Richard Hartley gave in to his growing concern and tried reaching his daughter by phone. When several attempts brought no reply, he got into his car and drove to the Rasmussen residence. There, a worrying scenario awaited him. No one answered when he knocked at the door. He then peered through a window, and could see one of Evelyn's canvas sneakers on the floor. His alarm now growing, Hartley circled the house, trying doors and windows. Eventually, he found an open basement window and gained entry. That was when he discovered blood spatters and clear signs of a struggle. The baby was there, and unharmed, but Evelyn was nowhere to be found.

The police officers who responded to Professor Hartley's frantic call were equally disconcerted by the scene. Not only was there blood inside the home, it tracked out over the lawn and away from the property. There was also a bloody hand print on a neighboring house, and the missing girl's other shoe, which was found in the basement. Investigators surmised that an intruder had gained access via the basement and that Evelyn had been overpowered when she had gone to investigate a noise. She had then been dragged away into the night

A massive search was conducted for Evelyn Hartley, eventually turning up bloodied clothing that had belonged to her. Other than that, no trace of her was ever found.

The disappearances of Georgia Weckler and Evelyn Hartley happened more than a hundred miles apart and there is no evidence that they were committed by the same perpetrator. Moreover, they occurred some distance from Plainfield and the victims, in each instance were children. Not so, the next three people to mysteriously drop off the face of the earth. First there was Victor Travis and Ray Burgess, a couple of deer hunters who ventured into the woods after a few too many drinks and vanished forever. Then there was Mary Hogan. The owner of Ed Gein's favorite watering hole.

On the afternoon of Wednesday, December 8, 1954, a farmer named Seymour Lester stopped off at Hogan's Tavern for a drink. To his surprise, he found the place deserted, an unusual state of affairs, particularly as the owner had failed to lock up the premises before she had departed. Lester was about to leave himself when he spotted a pool of blood behind the bar counter. That sent him sprinting for the door, scrambling into his truck and racing to the nearest farmhouse to call the police.

A short while later, Sherriff Howard S. Thompson arrived at the scene with a few of his deputies. It was immediately clear to the officers that Mary Hogan had met with foul play. The blood on the floor was streaked, as though someone had pulled her body through it, dragging it towards the door and then out into the parking lot. Moreover, the police found a spent .32-caliber shell. Mary had apparently been shot.

The question was, why? Robbery was ruled out as a motive since no attempt had been made to empty the register. It seemed that the killer had shot Mary Hogan then dragged her to the parking lot, loaded her into a pickup truck and driven away with her. But why? To what purpose? The police were left baffled as to the answer.

And they fared no better in locating the missing woman. A search of farms in the area yielded no result, while inquiries were made as far afield as Chicago, where Mary Hogan had previously lived. Nothing. Mary Hogan, like Georgia Weckler, like Evelyn Hartley, like Victor Travis and Ray Burgess, was gone. Her disappearance would remain a mystery for the next three years. Then it would be resolved in the most bizarre circumstances imaginable.

==========

The mystery of Mary Hogan's disappearance would be a topic of discussion around Plainfield for many years and none appeared more fascinated by it than Ed Gein. Ed, in fact, would develop a bizarre sense of humor about the case. His acquaintances, of course, knew that Ed had had a thing for Mary. They'd all seen him staring doe-eyed at her while barely sipping his beer. After Mary went missing, they began teasing him on the subject. On one occasion, a neighbor of Ed's named Elmo Ueeck teased him that if he'd plucked up the courage to ask Mary out, she'd be at his farmhouse right now, cooking dinner, rather than missing. "But she's not missing," Ed responded with a hint of humor in his voice. "She's down at the house right now." Ueeck, who like most folk around Plainfield thought that Ed was a few cards short of a full deck, could only chuckle.

On another occasion, Ed went even further. "I loaded her onto my pickup and drove her home," he said only half-jokingly." Again this elicited no more than wry chuckles and head shakes from the men who heard it. It was exactly what they'd come to expect from the local oddball.

Around this time, there was another story that began circulating about Ed Gein. The word was that he had a collection of shrunken heads in his house. Bob Hill, a local teenager who was on friendly terms with Gein, swore that he'd seen them. So too did some other kids who claimed to have snuck into the Gein farmhouse for a peek. Still, no one was particularly concerned about these rumors. Everyone knew that Ed was always telling tales about cannibals and headhunters. They assumed that the heads were Halloween decorations, bought by the little farmer to feed his obsession.

One can only imagine what the good citizens of Plainfield would have made of Ed's other "Halloween decoration," a suit he sometimes wore that made him look like the rotting corpse of an elderly woman. Sometimes, when the moon was full, he'd don this ghoulish get-up and cavort naked in his overgrown front yard.

Chapter 6: Hunting Season

The middle weeks of November are hunting season in Wisconsin, a nine-day window during which heavily-armed men descend on the woods and inflict wholesale slaughter on the local wildlife (and occasionally on one another). Ed Gein, however, was no hunter. In fact, he'd often professed that he was sickened by the sight of blood.

And so, as he headed into Plainfield on the drizzly afternoon of November 16, 1957, Ed was one of the few men around. That suited him just fine. The destination that he had in mind was Worden's Hardware Store. He planned on buying a quantity of anti-freeze there and had brought along a jug for that purpose.

Worden's was something of an institution in Plainfield. Founded in the 1890's as a harness shop, it had been acquired by Leon Worden in the 20's and had with the passage of time morphed into a general store that sold everything from farming equipment to household appliances to firearms. These days, it was run by Leon Worden's widow Bernice, who was usually assisted by her son, Frank. On the day in question, Frank (who also doubled as the town's deputy sheriff and fire warden) was out in the woods hunting, with the rest of the men. When Ed Gein entered the store carrying his glass jug, Bernice Worden was alone.

Bernice was less than pleased to see Ed. Generally, she did not have a problem with the scruffy little man but lately he'd been making a nuisance of himself, hanging around the store and pestering her to go to a movie with him, or to the roller rink in a neighboring town. Bernice wasn't certain if Ed meant the invitations seriously since he was wearing his perpetual grin when he made them. Still, she had no interest in stepping out with Ed Gein. Like most of the townsfolk, she regarded him as an idiot.

Today, however, all Ed wanted was a half-gallon of anti-freeze which Bernice pumped for him from the steel barrel that she kept in her office. She then took the dollar note he proffered, wrote out a sales receipt for 99c and handed him the receipt and his one cent in change. Ed then thanked her, picked up his jug and left.

But a moment later, Ed was back, having apparently deposited the jug of anti-freeze in his car. He'd been thinking, he told Bernice, of trading in his old Marlin rifle for a new one. Would it be okay if he checked out one of the Marlins hanging in the gun rack? Bernice said that that would be fine and removed the firearm Ed pointed out and handed it to him. While the little man began inspecting the weapon, she turned her back on him and looked out through the glass frontage into the street. While she was doing so, Ed was rooting around in his pockets, coming up with a .22 round and slotting it into the chamber. Bernice would not have seen him lift the rifle and draw a bead on the back of her head. She would not have heard the crack of the weapon or felt the impact of the bullet that ended her life.

At around five that evening, Frank Worden returned from his hunting excursion. It had been a cold and unproductive day in the woods and Frank was hardly in the best of spirits. And his mood was hardly improved when he arrived at the hardware store and found it shut. Hadn't his mother told him that she was keeping the store open until six? More to the point, why had she left all of the lights on? Feeling just a little annoyed Frank decided to stop by his house to pick up his set of store keys. He was back within a matter of minutes.

But the moment Frank stepped inside, he knew that something was wrong. The cash register was missing from the counter and there were brownish splatters on the floor which he recognized instantly as blood. Then he spotted the drag marks, also in blood, leading to the back door. Following them, he opened the door into the yard and saw that the store truck was missing.

Frank Worden was by now deeply concerned about his mother's wellbeing. But he was a trained deputy and so he managed to remain calm as he placed a call to Sheriff Art Schley at his office in Wautoma about fifteen miles away. Schley listened attentively as Worden described what he'd found. Then he told Worden to stay put until he arrived. After hanging up the phone, Schley called his chief deputy, Arnie Fritz. Some twenty minutes later, the two officers pulled up outside Worden's Hardware Store. Inside, they found a clearly distressed Frank Worden. "I know who did this," Worden said as they entered. He held up a rectangle of paper which the officers took to be a sales receipt. "Ed Gein," he said bitterly.

The sales receipt, Worden explained, was not the only reason that he suspected Gein. "He's been hanging around the store a lot lately," he said. "Pestering my mother to go out with him. Just yesterday he was in here asking if I'd be going hunting today. I didn't think much of it at the time but I'm wondering now if he planned on getting my mother alone."

Both Schley and Fritz agreed that Gein was a viable suspect and should be located as soon as possible. Before they went after him, however, they wanted to call in some backup. Fritz therefore got on the phone and started calling local jurisdictions. Before long, lawmen from as far afield as Madison were converging on the sleepy little burg of Plainfield. By early evening, the street outside Worden's Hardware Store was crammed with police cruisers of various descriptions, all of them with revolving blue and red roof lights. And the locals had also been drawn from their homes by the commotion. Plainfield had never seen anything like this in its entire history.

Ed Gein, meanwhile, was totally unaware of the furor. He was having dinner at the home of the Hill family, having been invited to stay after helping them get their car started. The first he heard of the hubbub going on downtown was when Irene Hill's son-in-law, Jim Vroman, rushed in and told them about it. Ed showed little reaction to the story, except to comment that it would have taken someone "pretty cold-hearted" to drag Bernice Worden away. He then agreed to drive Bob Hill downtown to see what was going on. He was sitting in his car, just about to leave the Hill residence, when Deputies Dan Chase and Poke Spees found him.

Gein made no objection when the officers asked him to accompany them to their squad car. He then willingly answered questions regarding his whereabouts that day but soon tripped himself up by insisting that he had nothing to do with Bernice Worden's death.

"How do you know that Mrs. Worden is dead?" Chase asked him.

"I heard it," Gein replied without a moment's hesitation.

"Heard it from who?" Chase persisted.

"I must have heard them talking about it," Gein said, without elaborating on who he was referring to.

Chase then informed him that he was a suspect in the robbery of Worden's Hardware Store and then radioed his chief to tell him that he had Ed in custody. Neither of them could have suspected at that time that they had just embarked upon one of the most sensational murder inquiries in American history.

Chapter 7: House of Horrors

Sherriff Arthur Schley had been in his position less than a month and this was the first major case he'd had to take charge of. He was less than certain of how to proceed but was pleased nonetheless at how things were going. After just a few hours, his men already had a suspect in custody. A suspect to what, though? Robbery certainly, since a cash register had been taken, along with the store truck and a brand new Marlin rifle. But Schley must have known that there was more to the case than that. The blood left at the scene suggested a far more serious offense. The next course of action was therefore clear. They had to find Bernice Worden.

The obvious place to start was Ed Gein's farmhouse and so Schley asked Captain Lloyd Schoephoerster of the Green Lake County Sheriff Department to accompany him and headed out of town, arriving a short while later at the ramshackle structure.

By moonlight, the Gein house had a sinister look to it, as though it kept secrets that might drive a man crazy were he to discover them. Even the police officers felt a chill as they tramped across the yard, a chill that had nothing to do with the frigid weather. With flashlight beams illuminating their path, the men rounded the property, trying doors and windows and finding all of them tightly shut. Then they reached the summer kitchen and at last found an entry.

Schoephoerster led the way, his beam picking a path across a floor littered with cartons, tins, moldering feed bags and other garbage. Cobwebs hung from the ceiling and on the counters roaches scurried to escape the light. From underfoot came the scuttling of rodents. The place gave off a quite sickening stench of damp and filth and offal gone bad. What kind of a person could live in these conditions, Schoephoerster wondered?

They were at the inter-leading door now, the one that gave entry into the house itself. Again the handle yielded when turned and this time Schley entered first, his flashlight picking out the details of a filthy and chaotic kitchen. All sorts of junk littered the floor, making in almost impossible to pick a path. And the smell in here was far worse, now it included the unmistakable stench of human waste and something else, the dull coppery aroma of freshly butchered meat.

Schley rounded a carton of mildewed newspapers and turned side-on to pick a path past a couple of rank and stained mattresses. The weatherworn floorboards creaked under his feet. Now he backed up against something that sent an involuntary spasm of revulsion through his body. Turning slowly and playing his beam across the object he was greeted by the sight of a decapitated and gutted carcass, suspended by its legs from the ceiling. For the briefest of moments Schley's brain registered an automatic response...deer. But then the reality of what he'd seen hit him and he turned and ran, blundering into the dark. He barely made it outside before he dropped to his knees and ejected the contents of his stomach into the snow. Bernice Worden had been found.

=======

It took more than a few minutes for Schoephoerster and Schley to steady their frayed nerves. Then Schoephoerster went to his squad car and reported what they'd found and he and Schley steeled themselves and re-entered the house. This time they were at least prepared for the horror that awaited them but that did not make the experience any less harrowing. The gutted, headless corpse had been suspended from a crude wooden crossbar fixed to the ceiling. A sharpened stake had been inserted through the ankle tendon of one leg to facilitate this, while the other leg was tied to the crossbar with a rope. The victim's arms were held against her body by another length of rope that ran from her wrists to the crossbar. A block-and-tackle had been used to hoist the body of the 58-year-old grandmother into this undignified position.

By now, the first of the backup officers had arrived and they too were left stunned by the sheer barbarity of the scene. But the butchered carcass of Bernice Worden was just the first of many horrors that they would uncover. Eddie Gein, the soft-spoken bachelor with the lopsided grin, the harmless old man who had acted as babysitter to many of their offspring, had been keeping secrets.

The first impression that the officers formed of the Gein homestead was that it was extremely filthy. Ed Gein seemed to regard his living quarters as a conveniently placed landfill. The floor was strewn with bottles, cans, scraps of partially eaten food, old newspapers, filthy rags, boxes of moldering magazines, rodent droppings, all of it giving off a noxious odor that had many of the officers gagging and protecting their sensitive nostrils by pinching them between thumb and forefinger. Then there were Gein's peculiar keepsakes – a Maxwell House coffee can containing lumps of masticated chewing gum, a collection of cracked and yellowed dentures, a washbasin which Gein had for some reason filled with sand and placed in the middle of the floor. All of these were strange but nothing compared to the rest of Ed's bizarre collection.

One of the officers picked up a crudely shaped soup bowl, still bearing the congealed remnants of Ed's last meal, then rapidly put it down when he realized what it was – the top half of a human skull. There were other skulls too, including some that were hung from the posts of Gein's bed as decoration. In the kitchen, Schoephoerster found a chair with oddly colored strips of leather forming the seat. Closer inspection proved that the "leather" was in fact made from strips of human skin, the underside still lumpy with chunks of fat.

Four such chairs were found in the house. So too, were other artifacts made from skin – a waste basket, lampshades, a drum, the sheath of a hunting knife, a belt made from female nipples, a shade pull made out of a pair of lips. Even these paled in comparison with Gein's most horrific creation – a "skin suit" consisting of a pair of leggings and a top piece that included a woman's sagging breasts. It appeared that Gein had skinned one of his victims, tanned the hide and then constructed this hideous ensemble. To what purpose? The officers shuddered to think but it seemed obvious that the little bachelor enjoyed wearing it.

Neither was this the last of the discoveries at the Gein house. In a box, officers found a collection of female genitalia, nine vulvas in all, most dried and shriveled but the latest addition sprinkled with salt to preserve it. There was also a box full of human noses and the pride of Eddie's collection – his death masks. These, the officers surmised, were what the teenagers had previously reported as "shrunken heads." It appeared that Gein had carefully peeled the skin from his victims' skulls and used a stuffing of paper and sawdust to give them shape. Four of these macabre objects were mounted on the wall. Others were stored inside plastic and paper bags and at least one of them was recognizable. "My god, it's Mary Hogan," one of the officers said.

The case of the missing innkeeper, gone for over three years, had finally been resolved. And if Gein had killed Bernice Worden and Mary Hogan, the police wondered, how many other women had he murdered? Judging by the number of body parts found in his home, quite a few.

There was one other area of the house that the police officers had yet to investigate and seeing as this area was sealed off, with planks of wood nailed across the doorway, the officers were apprehensive of what it might contain. Given the horrors that Gein had left in plain sight what might be so terrible that he felt it needed to be hidden from the world?

As it turned out, the sealed off area was a shrine. Augusta Gein's bedroom, covered in a generous layer of dust but otherwise neat as a pin. Ed had left it exactly as it had been on the day his beloved mother had died.

Chapter 8: The Body Snatcher

Following his arrest, Ed Gein was transported to the county jailhouse in Wautoma. There, he was questioned by Joe Wilimovsky, a polygraph specialist from the State Crime Lab. But despite being subjected to intense interrogation, Gein maintained a stoic silence for over twelve hours. When he eventually did start talking, he caught the investigators entirely by surprise. They believed that they had captured the worst mass murderer in the state's history but Gein had an altogether different, although no less horrific, tale to tell.

He admitted killing Bernice Worden, although he claimed that it had been an accident. According to Gein, he'd been trying the Marlin rifle to see if it would accommodate the .22 ammo he had when the weapon had accidentally discharged, hitting Mrs. Worden in the head. He couldn't remember all the details, he said, because it happened in a daze. However, he vaguely remembered dragging the body outside and loading it into the store truck. He'd then driven the truck a short distance out of town, hidden it in some trees and returned to pick up his car. Mrs. Worden's body was later transferred from the truck to the car and driven out to the Gein farmhouse. There he had begun butchering the corpse but had been interrupted when Bob Hill had knocked on his door and asked for his help in getting the Hill family car started. Gein had then gone to the Hill residence and had later enjoyed a meal with the family, while Bernice Worden's desecrated corpse was hanging upside down in his kitchen. He was still at the Hills when the police arrived to arrest him.

Gein had delivered this confession in a deadpan way that was at odds with the silly little grin that remained fixed to his face throughout. However, the investigators were far from satisfied with his explanation. If it really had been an accident, they wanted to know, why hadn't he just called the police? Why had he chosen to haul the body away? Why had he butchered it? On those issues Gein again claimed amnesia. "It's all very hazy," he said.

The interrogators could see that they were not going to get anything else from Gein regarding the Worden murder so they tried another tack. What about the other bodies that had been found at the farmhouse, estimated by now to be the remains of at least ten women? What of Mary Hogan, the one victim who had thus far been identified? Here, Gein's answer caught them by surprise. He admitted to killing Hogan although his version of events was almost identical to his telling of the Worden murder. He said that he'd been sitting at the bar in Hogan's Tavern when his rifle had accidentally discharged and the bullet had hit the innkeeper in the head. Since Ed was the lone customer in the tavern at the time, he'd decided to haul the body away to cover up what had happened. As for the other bodies the police had found, he said that they were not murder victims but corpses he'd stolen from local cemeteries.

Bizarre as the case had thus far proven to be, the officers were stunned by this latest admission. They were also disinclined to believe it. It seemed impossible that a man of Gein's stature could dig up a corpse, drag it from its casket and then fill in the grave again, all in the few hours he'd have had to complete the task.

But Gien was insistent, even providing the officers with a list of the graves he'd robbed. His M.O., he said, was to follow the obituaries in local newspapers, looking for middle-aged women who had recently died. He'd then visit the graveyard late at night and get to work. The soil in the newly dug grave was still loose and that made the digging easy. Besides, Ed said with his trademark grin, he never had to dig the full six-feet. All of the coffins were encased in a wooden box, the lid of which was usually two feet below the surface. All he had to do was pry up the boards with a crowbar and he was in business. Sometimes, he'd carry the whole corpse away with him. On other occasions, he'd cut off the head and leave the body behind.

Once Gein had the desired body parts in hand, he'd return to his filthy farmhouse where he'd spend hours cutting and dissecting the corpse, creating the macabre artifacts that would later be found in his house. He'd then burn the rest of the body although, on a few occasions, he'd suffered the pangs of conscience and had returned the mutilated remains to the cemetery, where he'd buried them. He insisted that all of this was true although few of the officers believed him. They were still convinced that they had captured the worst serial killer in Wisconsin's history.

In the midst of the storm brewing around him, Ed Gein appeared totally oblivious to the enormity of the crimes he'd committed. But by now stories about the macabre case had begun to leak out, alerting the media. Soon a frenzy would be whipped up with reporters from around the country descending on the hitherto unknown burg of Plainfield and on Wautoma where Gein was being held. Ed Gein, the shy little farmer from Wisconsin was suddenly a celebrity, with newsmen and TV crews besieging the jailhouse, hoping to get a shot of the diminutive ghoul. Any effort to move him from one location to another became an ordeal for the lawmen assigned to his case. They were immediately tracked by a convoy of a dozen cars, with any glimpse of Gein triggering a blizzard of flashbulbs.

Over the weeks that followed, Gein's grinning countenance could be seen staring out from newspapers across the land. He even appeared on the cover of magazines like Time and Life. Meanwhile, some of the country's most renowned psychiatrists offered their opinion on what made Ed tick and there was a new Gein-inspired phenomenon, a rash of distasteful but popular jokes, known as "Geiners." One example went like this: "Why did they let Ed Gein out of prison on New Year's Eve?" "So he could dig up a date."

Back in Plainfield, residents were inundated with reporters, all of them keen to find the next new shocking twist in the Gein saga. Most Plainfielders resented the intrusion but some did speak to the press and others were happy to spin wild yarns which were instantly accepted as fact. The press also added their own spin. There were suggestions that Gein had had sex with the corpses he dug up (Ed denied this, saying that they smelled too bad). There were also unsubstantiated allegations of cannibalism (also denied by Gein). The Gein farmhouse, meanwhile, had become somewhat of a tourist attraction, with rubberneckers driving from all over the region just to catch a glimpse of the dilapidated old building.

In the midst of all this mayhem, permission was finally granted to dig up the graves Gein claimed to have robbed. This would answer once and for all the question of whether Ed Gein was a double murderer and grave robber or the prolific serial killer that law enforcement officers believed him to be.

The first of the graves cited for exhumation was that of Mrs. Eleanor Adams, and its location was telling. It was right next to that of Augusta Gein, Ed's beloved mother. On the chilly morning of Monday, November 24, police and workmen descended on the Plainfield cemetery. District Attorney Earl Kileen had earlier announced that the evacuations would begin on Tuesday and so the army of newsmen encamped in Plainfield was caught entirely by surprise. Those who figured out that something was up arrived at the cemetery to find their way blocked and the grave itself screened off by a tarpaulin. Behind that screen, two workmen had already started digging.

After less than an hour, the shovels scraped against the top of the rough wooden box that encased the coffin. And it was immediately clear that the box had indeed been tampered with. The wood had been splintered. As for the coffin itself, it lay four feet below, a scattering of dirt on the lid. One of the workmen lowered himself into the hole and flipped back the lid as all of those present held a collective breath. The casket was empty. It was so with every coffin they dug up, save for those where Gein had taken the head and left the body behind or where he had, out of conscience, returned the mutilated remains to their final resting place.

Chapter 9: Psycho

And so Ed Gein's stories of late night visits to the graveyard turned out to be true after all. Grave robbing was still a crime, of course, but not as serious a crime as murder. Ed still had two homicides to answer for. But the question plaguing D.A. Kileen was whether he'd be able to prosecute Gein at all. Already Gein's defense counsel had stated his intention of pursuing an insanity defense and it seemed highly likely that such a defense would succeed. Surely a man who dug up and mutilated corpses, holding their body parts as keepsakes, had to be insane? It was an issue that needed to be resolved before the matter could be brought before a jury.

Gein was therefore sent to the Central State Hospital for the Criminally Insane where a month's worth of tests by various experts delivered the inevitable verdict. Ed Gein was found to be mentally incompetent. "Mr. Gein has been suffering from a schizophrenic process for an undetermined period of years," wrote Central State Hospital director, Dr. Edward Schubert. "Although Mr. Gein might voice knowledge of the difference between right and wrong, his ability to make such judgment will always be influenced by the existent mental illness. As a result of these findings, I must recommend his commitment to Central State Hospital as insane."

And that, indeed, was the ruling of the court. Much to the disgust of the citizens of Plainfield, Gein was deemed to be criminally insane and was sent back to Central State, having never been called on to answer for his crimes. He adapted well to institutional life. To a man who had spent most of his adult life living in a grim and filthy farmhouse, the assurance of three hot meals a day and a warm cot at night must have seemed like Nirvana. He had clean clothes, medical care, even a small television set in his room. To the people of Plainfield, it must have appeared that Ed Gein had not only gotten away with murder but had profited from it. Perhaps that simmering resentment is what led to the fire at the Gein farm.

Shortly after Gein was sent to Central State, an auction was scheduled to sell off his farm and other belongings. Ed, of course, would see very little, if any, of the proceeds. He had legal bills to pay as well as civil suits that had been lodged by the families of his victims. Still, the auction attracted considerable interest, both from serious bidders and from the morbidly curious.

One item that would not end up under the auctioneer's hammer was the farmhouse itself. In the early morning hours of March 20, 1958, the Plainfield volunteer fire department was called out to the Gein farm where they found the house ablaze and already beyond rescue. The firemen stood impassively by as the building burned to the ground. Arson was suspected but the town fire warden, Bernice Worden's son Frank, was disinclined to launch an inquiry. When Ed was told about the destruction of his family home, he was equally pragmatic. "Just as well," he said without emotion.

As for the rest of Gein's possessions, the farm sold to a property investor for around $3,000 and the rest sold for a pittance. One item, however, provoked a bidding war. It was Ed's 1949 Ford sedan, the vehicle which he'd used to haul disinterred corpses back home. It sold eventually for $760 to a sideshow operator named Bunny Gibbons. That would prove to be a shrewd investment. For years after, Gibbons toured the Midwest, exhibiting the "ghoul car" at a quarter a peek. It seemed that people just could not get enough of the Plainfield Butcher.

As for the object of their fascination, he was doing well at the hospital where he was described as a model prisoner. And he was responding well to therapy. So well, in fact, that in January 1968, ten years after he'd begun his incarceration, a court decided that he was now competent to stand trial for the murder of Bernice Worden.

Those proceedings got underway on November 7, 1968, with much of the testimony given over to gruesome autopsy reports and evidence by lawmen who had been involved in the original investigation, many of who had since retired. One notable absentee was Sheriff Art Schley, who had dropped dead of a heart attack just months before the trial was due to begin.

Gein himself was the main defense witness and even though a decade had passed since the murder, he was still sticking to his story that Bernice Worden's death had been an accident.

Gein's defense team had opted to waive his right to a jury trial, so it was up to Judge Robert H. Gollmar to decide on his guilt or innocence. And since Gein continued to insist that the shooting had been an accident, the judge had no difficulty in returning a guilty verdict. The outcome, however, was purely academic. Gein had been found to be mentally incompetent at the time of the shooting and thus could not be sentenced to jail time. Judge Gollmar ruled instead that he should be returned to the Central State Hospital for the Criminally Insane and should remain there for an indeterminate period. The possibility of release at some later date was not ruled out.

Ed was pleased at the outcome. He was happy at the hospital. He got along well with the staff and well enough with the other patients, even though he preferred to keep to himself. He'd put some weight on his scrawny frame and was in better condition physically than he'd been since his youth. He remained an avid reader even though his favorite material – Nazi atrocities and cannibal massacres – was off the menu. He enjoyed his regular chats with the psychologists and was keen on the occupational therapy projects he participated in. He even earned a small income by cleaning the wards and was allowed to spend his money on an inexpensive ham radio set. All in all, Gein was probably happier during his last decade and a half than he'd been at any time during his life.

Ed Gein died of respiratory failure on July 26, 1984, at the age of 78. By then he was senile and riddled with cancer. In accordance with his wishes, he was buried at the Plainfield cemetery beside his beloved mother. His grave is unmarked to discourage sightseers and vandals. Ironically, Ed lies buried close to the very graves that he so heartlessly plundered.

The Butcher of Plainfield was gone but the enormity of his crimes was not forgotten. Over the years that followed he would continue to be the bogeyman that Wisconsin mothers warned their misbehaving children about. And he would continue to inspire writers and movie makers. In addition to the character Buffalo Bill, mentioned in the intro of this book, Gein was also the inspiration for Leatherface, the chainsaw-wielding maniac in Tobe Hooper's 1974 horror classic, The Texas Chainsaw Massacre, the film which launched the 'Slasher' subgenre.

But perhaps the most famous of Ed Gein's fictional incarnations was Norman Bates, the cross-dressing, mother-obsessed Psycho of Robert Bloch's novel and Alfred Hitchcock's classic film. Each of these characters, Buffalo Bill, Leatherface and Norman Bates draws on Ed Gein. And yet the atrocities committed by Gein were far more bizarre, far more extreme than those of his fictional counterparts. Fact, in this case, really was stranger than fiction.

For more True Crime books by Robert Keller please visit

http://bit.ly/kellerbooks

Printed in Great Britain
by Amazon